THE ART OF
INSPIRATION

CHERYL,

FROM THE DAYS of "WATERMELON"!
I SAY THANK YOU! MAY YOU
CONTINUE YOUR JOURNEY of light
AND LOVE!

MANY BLESSING MY FRIEND!

Kris

THE ART OF
INSPIRATION

Affirmations for
Spiritual Awareness

KRIS WHITE

BALBOA
PRESS

A DIVISION OF HAY HOUSE

Balboa Press books may be ordered through booksellers or by contacting:

Balboa Press
A Division of Hay House
1663 Liberty Drive
Bloomington, IN 47403
www.balboapress.com
1-(877) 407-4847

ISBN: 978-1-4525-3527-2 (sc)
ISBN: 978-1-4525-3566-1 (e)

Library of Congress Control Number: 2011908902

Printed in the United States of America

Balboa Press rev. date: 6/13/2011

For
Ashley Howard-White and Carmela Trembley

Many thanks to Darwin White, Michele English, and Shana Mislak. Their belief and motivation have given me the fortitude to follow my dream of writing.

With much gratitude for the many people who have inspired these writings during our sessions throughout the years together.

CONTENTS

INTRODUCTION

Daily affirmations are a wonderful way to release the hold the mind has over the control of an individual. It's a way to speak aloud positive affirmations, release the old patterns formulated in life, and create positive reinforcement that is practiced by many successful people.

If you find yourself in a need of a mood stabilizer, an epiphany, encouragement, or enlightenment, then this is the book for you.

The Art of Inspiration was written to help the reader tap into their intuitive self while letting go of unsupportive behaviors. The mix of prayers and affirmations help generate an enlightened undertone in order to break the deeper current of negativity. *The Art of Inspiration* can be read in a sequence of chapters, or you can simply open to a page and let it speak to you in the moment.

PRAYER AND AFFIRMATION

$\mathcal{W}$e should be giving God our glory instead of submitting our complaint list.

*T*oday, I am graced with another waking day. The grace of God has blessed me with another chance to accomplish extraordinary moments that can happen within a day's time. Whether this is my first or my last, I wish to make the best of this day.

$\mathcal{M}$ay the powers that be awaken passiveness inside of me. Lend me a moment of calmness so that I may see my direction more clearly and not get caught in the drama that continually confuses me.

Believe

Believe in yourself when no one else can.

Believe in yourself when you feel lost and alone.

Believe in yourself when you can't make a stand.

Believe in yourself when you feel you have failed.

Believe in yourself when there is no one to guide you.

Believe in yourself no matter what you do.

Believe in the mere fact that you are here on this earth to believe in you.

Dear God,

Lift me out of these trying times. Help me to focus my thoughts and let go of my anxiety around my current situation. Assist me in moving myself forward and allow me comfort in knowing as this moment passes, a moment of clarity is on the horizon.

Today

I open to my earthly desires to bring balance to my daily experiences.

I am connected to who I am as an individual, relinquishing to the possibility that my soul has lived before, living in the now and acquiring patience for the moment.

As a human upon my journey, I let go of all my ideas of how my life should or should not be.

I accept I was born into this journey to unfold my individual quest of life and lessons. With this privilege of life comes the responsibility to unfolding a life with purpose and growth.

I will continue to honor the source from which my life was given. In doing so I resolve that the value of my day evolves through the power of each moment, creating collective moments essential to my daily destiny.

Living in my truths means I am to develop stillness to be able to recognize my truths. I trust in the plan I created for myself long ago. I challenge myself to let go of my past hurts and failures, those disappointments and sorrows that I have carried within my body and mind. I am ready to release these pains that have swayed me into living with a heavy heart, burdens that were meant to be released and woes that no longer belong to me. My goals are happiness and the clarity to see myself as I truly am. I am freeing myself from all those judgments that have limited me over the years. Today, I am developing a keener vision of myself—one that needs not be viewed through a limited vision of the person I am. These visions of a lesser person have suited me for a period of time within my life. No more do I wish to carry these negative images. Today, I view myself as whole person living my life in my God-like image.

Dear God,

My heart is guarded, my mind holds much disbelief, and my life is a creation of troubled moments. Yet I am in my glory and grace with our connection. I refuse to let these trying moments sway me away from you. I find power in our connection and faith in your creation of me. I will no longer allow myself to play victim to my life. I will continue to marvel in the light of my life and follow the darkness until I find my brighter day. Bless me with your love and continue to guide me as I travel forward into my day.

I Am a Magnet

I am a magnet to my divine inheritance. I draw to me the abundance of my divine birthright. I am open to gather all my earthly treasures reserved for me in this life. In this lifetime I shall manifest all that is mine.

*H*elp free me from the limits of my personality. Open my mind to a level of understanding that will move my thoughts beyond my daily limitations.

I am confident that my soul is securely fitted to my human body. I am bound in flesh, yet I have no limitations from within. The freedom of my person as the individual I am is limitless. I am bountiful in spirit and therefore graced as a human. Any resistance comes not from my embodiment but from the limits I secrete through my mind. Confidence is not derived from another—my confidence is derived from the depths of my soul.

I relinquish all my fears, insecurities, and inadequacies to the unseen powers of the universe. I strengthen my person by walking my talk and not wavering in my faith. No matter how bumpy my path, I believe in the powers I cannot see. For this, I feel confident that I am being guided and directed through my daily life.

*A*llow me a moment of secure footing upon this earth. Bless me with internal wisdom while humbling me into grace and goodness with my life. Reward me with peace of mind as I embark upon my daily tasks.

*B*ring me peace within my day, happiness within my heart, and clarity within my thoughts. Guide me into a day of joyous behaviors. Allow me to encounter the power of the universe as I walk forward along my path. Protect me from the banter of my negative thoughts. Support me throughout my day with peace of mind. Allow me to flow with my strengths, lessen my struggles, and gain control over my fear as I journey into the beginning of today.

*M*y heart seems hardened from all my negative experiences I have participated in throughout my life. Because of great loss, disappointments, shame, embarrassment, and lack of success, I am living unattached to my life. Yet in this moment I am willing to let go of these negative perceptions and accept those times have allowed me to grow within my life. Without the turbulence I would not have evolved into the person I am today: stronger, wiser, and more compassionate towards others. I am trying to release my anger toward my failures so I may lend a positive outlook to my struggles. Help me release my anger and feel free of my frustrations so that I may grow within this very second of my unsettledness.

I no longer chose to second-guess my every action. I rise above my confusion and struggle by empowering my person. I let go of my negative perceptions and turn my thoughts toward positive awareness. I tap into my divine inner power so that I can lead my mind out of the shadows my thoughts have created. I will illuminate my inner being to trust in my God and hand over my insecurities. I believe in the grand powers of the unseen. I trust that this moment will lend to a new adventure that is less than trying. As I lift the veil of shadow in my mind, I begin to adjust to the light that will lead me into my inner salvation.

By exposing my insecurities, I shall silence my thoughts. By exploring my life I will follow a spiritual path. In order to live my destiny, I must trust and live from my heart.

I am who I am. If I can look into a mirror and see me as I am, then I can begin to believe I am worth understanding. If I can become comfortable with whom I am, then it's possible I may grow to be me.

I am open and am in the flow of my abundant, prosperous life. I am aware and ready for new opportunities to present themselves in my life. I am growing with insight and developing a clearer vision of where my life should be. Today, I seek guidance because I may limit myself with worry that my visions are not what are meant to be. I will remain open and patient that all will present itself to me in the appropriate moment. Just for now, I will release my worry and trust in the development of my visions.

*T*he most valued realization is when one understands the only person who has control is one's self.

$\mathcal{F}$inding a space to hold my own when everything within me feels alone.

Taking myself to this level of despair continually leaves me unaware.

When I trust that this moment is meant to be, I will open to the flow of all the things the universe will send to me.

If I close my mind to what is true, I limit myself to the world that shall lead me to you.

*M*y heart is heavy, my confidence low. I have faith in your guidance, but I am confused as which way I should go. If I stand still, it only triggers my pain. If I step forward, I feel as though I am walking on shaky ground. If I sit and wait, I am idling in wasted time. I wish I could hear you tell me what I should do. I believe your words would move me in one direction. It's hard to focus when I feel so stuck. I am desperate to do what is right by you and good for me, but I need a sign to keep me from putting myself in harm's way. I have spoken my thoughts aloud to you; now I will just keep moving forward to so that you will be able to get through with a thought, a word, or a sign or two. I know you won't let me down—not even in this moment that is too hard to handle. I will continue to manage until you show me what to do.

Forgiveness of my insecurities, lightness of my divine mind, and happiness within my heart equals true awareness in life. Release within me my troubled mind so that I may rejoice in my life as it is. Carry me forward with each new day until I am ready to let go of my past. Motivate me to be accountable for my efforts and live my life respectfully until the day I am called to leave this earth. May I continue to make every effort to better myself without the need for validation. Help me unfold each given day with a new awareness of the life I have chosen to live.

Blessed Be the Day

Blessed be the day I relinquish my struggles and take charge of my life. Blessed be the day I discover I have the strength to embrace my life through my challenges, which will expose my hidden power. Blessed be the day I extend my inner joy to all living creatures. Blessed be the day I share a simple smile with a stranger. Blessed be the day I gain control of my life, only to connect with my destiny. Blessed be the day I was born unto this earthly experience to find my individual expression of life.

Open

I am open to receive a love that will last.

I am open to embrace all opportunities with deeper gratitude.

I am open to learn from my life in this moment.

I am available to receive all that life is choosing to share with me.

I am intuitive in knowing the more connected I am to my life, the more my life will present back to me.

Courage of Speech

At times I find myself shy. In this moment, I am seeking to connect with my voice and understand why it is that I seem not to speak my feelings or truths as easily as I should.

I ask myself where my words are. I question if looking deeper would help me find my voice. Most times my emotions are mute because I cannot articulate my feelings.

When I sit in my silence and try to connect my words to my feelings within, I sense my words are not important enough.

I strain to find my confidence, yet my words do not appear. I am waiting to find the courage to speak so that I feel less than fear.

To become comfortable unleashing my words, I must speak because silence is no longer my friend. I have regressed myself back to the days of feeling young and immature.

I linger awhile to connect with my emotions and true feelings, finding that my voice is not a tone or lyric; it's the voice that lives within me.

I have the courage to speak and release my feelings. Finding my connection to speech lifts me out of my ambivalence and into using the spoken word. No longer shall I be muted in fear. I am open to using my voice, no matter who chooses to hear.

*T*he skill of learning patience lies in the art of not doing. This means allowing situations to reveal themselves in their own time without the push or pull for an outcome. Most times the outcome is not the one we may seek, yet it is the outcome that is in our highest good. Acceptance that we always receive exactly what we need will release the level of disappointment that is created when we don't receive what we perceive to be in our best interest.

LIFE AND INSPIRATION

*T*he pursuit of happiness requires the art of trying. The pursuit of life requires the art of living. An abundant life requires a life of pursuit.

Balance

For every up there is a down.

For every wet there is a dry.

For every good there is a bad.

For every tear there is a smile.

For every chuckle there is a sigh.

*U*nderstanding the creation of you and your life means accepting that limitations and flaws are a part of one's creation. Imperfection is perfection.

*Used to be*s are no more. It's time to move on with your life. Let go of that aspect of life that has you locked in and pining. It's in your past. Now move yourself along. There is another more important avenue of life to venture into and memories to be made. *Used to be*s are no more.

All the things in life you may believe to be unsolvable are in fact the most solvable. It merely takes a moment of refocusing to see the good of the situation as opposed to the bad of it.

Karma isn't something bad that is going to get the best of you in this life for a wrongdoing. Karma is merely an unresolved issue that one must complete in the present lifetime.

*L*iving in a life filled with the past keeps you stuck in yesterday. Living in the life of the present keeps you living toward the opportunities of tomorrow.

*C*oincidences are unimaginable moments that contain the surprise powers of the unknown.

A shadowed life is one of majestic light in reverse. One must be able to see the glory that exists in the moment that was created in darkness.

To have a serendipitous affair with life, you must live with an open mind and an adventurous heart.

$\mathcal{M}$ediocre lives are those lived wanting what other people have, instead of dreaming and creating what makes you thrive.

*W*hen we at least make an attempt in life, we are more apt to follow through within our life.

*S*ometimes situations in life get us so riled up that we have a tendency to forget the importance of life lies in the gift of living.

Compassion for Youth

In this world, bridges connect us from land to land, and we are able to transcend an open space.

In this world, people do meet in time to finish whatever journey they need to complete.

In this world, destiny does provide a life of living formed between earth and sky. In this world of life it is true: we lived best when we live by the golden rule; treat others as you wish to be treated yourself.

Our youth are our future. Guidance is one of the most important aspects needed by those who are growing. Influence helps them decide what is right and wrong. Patience allows them room to grow, a tender moment of truth lends them the knowledge they are supported. Honesty and compassion help them find clarity when searching for direction.

Goodness is viewed through kindness and communication. It is everyone's responsibility to protect our future by being present and available for our youth.

Being present means being responsible for the actions we take when in the presence of those more impressionable - our future, our youth.

As we grow older, life has a tendency to move more quickly. With life seemingly moving faster, we are challenged to create more, focus less on the time that has passed, and pay more attention to one's life in the present time. This will not slow life from its sped up pace; rather, it will simply help you savor the moments of the life that is ahead and not the life that has been left behind.

RELATIONSHIP

When searching for a relationship, remember the old cliché "there is a lid for every pot." You just have to be open to finding the right lid and not judging the pot. It takes more than a second of observation to see if a person is truly the right person for you. Judging the outside discounts the beauty inside.

Take My Hand

Long ago in heaven's place, you took my hand and made me a promise to find each other on the earth below.

I went first—my journey I did not fear. In my soul I always kept you near.

Our love was strong. At times my journey seemed quite long. No matter who I met or where I traveled, deep within I was convinced you would one day come along.

With each step I took, I felt closer to you within my heart. Ours is a love I knew would never part, as it was blessed in heaven above. A true blessing to find, you will not be an end of such a gift of unconditional love.

At times the reality of you seemed as lucid as a dream. My faith I wished to waver; at times my heart felt you were not true. Yet, my soul was certain somewhere you existed.

I traveled along in my life with a hope that someday you would appear, that you would be my truth, that one day, the reality of you would present yourself to me. Not a moment too soon.

Now we are here. My heart knows it's you, and the day we first met my soul knew it too.

Our connection, our love is the light that touches my inner being. The existence through our connection now makes my life whole.

Let our story keep unfolding as we grow together, as we grow old. Let there never be a day that your heart is not connected to my soul.

Take my hand, as I place mine in yours. Take my heart because we never wish to part. For our story is now witnessed, our love is now committed to being true.

Take my hand, and I shall never leave you.

RELATIONSHIP

The heart dare not hide a genuine aspect of one's soul. A soft place that holds no judgment should be honored.

$\mathcal{I}$f you wish to gain respect, you have to be willing to give respect.

*W*hat is at the crux of an argument? A point that is trying to be understood. In order to understand another, one has to realize there are at least two ways to solve a problem. No one answer gives us the solution; it's a union of thoughts and opinions that lead us to the resolve.

Love is a simple word chosen to express the deep, subtle emotion from one's heart—when in reality, love is the freedom that lives in kindness.

*N*ot every conversation has to be won. Listening more than speaking lessens the ego's response and leads to a more mature level of understanding others.

*W*e as humans need a sense of belonging, a defining of our self-worth and existence. To understand our needs, we must first be willing to let go of our wants. True desires make up a deeper understanding of the whole of humankind, the evolution of one's life. Being a part of life allows us to continually work on finding our best selves. When we can accept our shortcomings, we can begin to uncover our trueness.

*A*llow others to be as they are; then you are free to finding your own way to be.

A selfless act is the simple gesture of human awareness.

*F*ocusing on the lives of others causes us to lose sight of our own visions and gifts. Wanting what belongs to someone else's life limits us from our divine inheritance.

*C*onversational mishaps only happen when we are listening with an agenda. Only when we listen with the intention to listen are we truly present to hear.

Getting to know another takes more than a glance; it's the time spent around someone that unfolds the true essence of the person. Time spent is a gentle reminder it's more than a moment that formulates a bond.

*K*indred souls bring the feeling of happiness through togetherness. Life is meant to be lived through interaction with others. Our connection to others brings joy to the heart and recognition to the soul. Even the most trying of moments brings growth to both lives.

*L*aughter is our soul's tone. No one sound is the same. Yet when we experience another's laughter and its unique vibration, we can't help but smile.

*A*nger: a wasted level of self-centeredness, the rejection of kindness, kin to frustration, brother of arrogance and sister to self-ignorance, friend to insecurity.

*C*ompassion derives from the depths of truth, a truth only the soul may recognize. Compassion is not control; it is the freedom within to give openly without expectation.

*A*s I grow older, my days grow shorter. I become wiser and more mature, having spent more time down on this earth with each passing year.

To value another, you must value yourself.

To love another, you must love yourself.

To honor another, you must honor yourself.

To respect another, you must respect yourself.

To change the world, you must start with yourself.

She

She, warmth of soul and strength of compassion.

She, moves gracefully through the freedom of dance.

She, the creator of life lived without limitation, an invitation to wholeness.

She, the one connected to the powers of life through kindness and forgiving words.

She, carries herself eloquently through turbulent times.

She, embraces obstacles with open arms, from her genuine connection to her faith.

She, loves unconditionally, even when she feels she is alone.

She, weeps for all of humankind and prays for peace for all as she weeps.

She, offers wisdom for those on an enlightened path.

She, dawns herself in light as she ventures through dark times.

She, the one connected to the universal forces through her forgiveness.

She, who softly embraces all aspects of life.

She, the other half of he.

He

He, takes a stand with his external power.

He, walks his path with an assertiveness to shield his vulnerabilities.

He, has the courage to forge ahead with his internal beliefs, protected by his masculine exterior.

He, the one who will not let himself fail based on society's views of his masculine form.

He, who finds his balance in life by using his voice of persuasion opposed to a push for power.

He, who allows himself to cry and feels his vulnerability through his masculinity.

He, who when faced with sorrow grieves in silence.

He, the one who leads others through crisis, knowing the unity will get the problem solved.

He, who knows a connection to the divine allows him to be strong for the community.

He, lends the broad of his shoulder to lean upon.

He, the other half of she.

Soul's Dance

In this moment I have forgotten the beauty of my life. I have placed myself in a rut and claimed it as unhappiness.

I must remember to acknowledge this moment and recognize that every slide forward will also slide me backward.

Our soul's dance requires inconsistency so that its human side may develop with life's dance. The personality needs a moment to understand there is no drudging through life's lessons—just flowing.

Just start with one step forward and let it lead you in the direction your soul wishes to take you.

GROWTH AND AWARENESS

When you find yourself in a moment of insecurity, remind yourself that what doesn't kill you only makes you stronger. Then and only then will you have the courage to move yourself out of your insecurities.

*B*laming others for our mishaps is a defeatist act of human nature. Succumbing to our insecurities and pointing the finger means we are limiting ourselves. Taking responsibility for one's own actions lends maturity to the human growth process.

The soul is protected by the human shell. There is weakness to the advancement of the soul when a person is abusing the protector, their human body. Taking care of the body gives support to the mind, which in turn advances the soul. When all are in balance; there is no limitation to the development of the whole being.

*B*oredom is a person's inadequacy staring them in the face. It is the sin that casts a shadow over our moments and wreaks havoc on our psyche.

$\mathcal{K}$indness is a response that happens naturally.

*P*lacating an uncomfortable conversation diffuses the moment. Learning to stay present and to speak up for yourself during those moments of uneasiness will allow you to master taking care of yourself.

*E*ven in our darkest moments, we are allotted growth.

To support your life, you must be able to speak truth directly from your soul—no matter how the world responds to your words. If you offer the world a new vision, then there will be some that will begin to listen. If you offer the world negative banter, then you are not only doing a disservice to yourself, but to the world around you.

*W*hen we get caught up with the outside world, we fall short of our individual journey.

We have designed our bodies to house our soul. If our house is of ill health, the soul is not being supported. If our soul is not of good care, then our journey will seem sluggish.

Failures are moments of growth for the personality, a test to achieve and override the challenge of the disappointment. For some this comes naturally. For others, they will repeat the disappointment until they see the failure not as a challenge but an advancement of the personality.

If your thoughts are full of concern, your heart filled with imbalance, your path layered with obstacles, your vision blurred, and your world hopeless, then keep moving yourself through your insecurities and trust that these moments are filled with higher purpose. When you have moved yourself through the moment, you will have succeeded with inner growth.

$\mathcal{D}$isliking life means you need to push yourself through the moment to find a greater level of understanding of the world around you.

*J*udgment holds no light. Guidance should be offered without control.

When we create the story before the story is created, we are implying we know the outcome of something that has not yet come to pass.

*N*ot everything done to excess is healthy. Limiting the quantity of your choices means you are free to experience more.

Choices

There is no power in shadow without the light. There is no power in light without shadow.

Balance is the combination of both forces. One may have chosen a life of light but has spent a considerable period of life healing the shadow side of one's soul.

The process will reverse itself if the choice of shadow has been chosen. At one point, even when the human is nearing death, the soul may shine a light right before the last breath.

Turbulence in one's mind rattles around like forced steam through an old radiator. To release the steam, one must find a way to relinquish the vapor and breathe.

*W*e spend too much of our time focusing on life as it used to be or should be. Instead, we should focus our thoughts and conversations on how life is in this very moment.

SILENCING THE MIND

*C*learing the chatter within your mind means trusting there is something more important with which to fill your mind.

*I*nstability wreaks havoc on the mind, and spinning one's wheels brings total insanity. Silencing the mind creates inner peace. Creating silence only happens when you step away from your insanity and focus yourself on something else.

*W*hen one's mind becomes consumed with daily tasks, take a moment to step out into nature. These moments of freedom will allow clarity upon reentry to the day and one's task.

A prescient mind sees through the veil of the unknown. There is no struggle when everything unseen is seen.

*W*hen you allow your mind to run interference with your heart, you will live in a state of frustration and confusion.

*W*ithin this moment is how we can accomplish our life's goals.

$\mathcal{F}$reedom arises within our individual mind-set once we realize everything isn't about us. Life is about the unity of the collectiveness.

When the mind suggests there is a limit within our reach for what we wish to obtain, then the body will cease to extend itself past the extension. Yet when the mind is not focused on restraint, the reach continues to be limitless. Our only humanistic limits exist within the lack of extending our thought process.

*S*tillness is a beat of silence from deep within the soul. All your answers will come when you are able to still the mind and follow the rhythms of your soul.

Inner Voice

Deep within the human core lives our voice. We are all born with an inner voice that strengthens and develops over a period of a lifetime.

Finding one's voice requires the confidence to speak openly whenever is suitable. Everyday experiences are constant reminders our words have value. Muting such a powerful aspect of self will lend frustration to one's life.

Developing an inner voice takes time and maturity. Like all else, we have to be responsible for the words we chose to speak. When we develop such a powerful tool as our voice, we become responsible not only to those we encounter, but also for the conversations we choose to hold.

Reflections of our thoughts are our words. The development of one's inner voice needs to be a reflection of one's true self. If we develop our voice from a false sense of pride, we run the risk of developing a voice of arrogance which in turn is foreseen as ignorance.

For a strong and responsive inner voice, we must choose to live a life with an open mind and clear voice, not a life based on opinion or judgment.

A mind can create visions of reality based on individual beliefs. This truth may be far from another's reality, yet no human should doubt another's truth based on fact or fiction. When we allow a person to hold their own truth, whether stated right or wrong, we are allowing that person their own journey. If their truths do not match yours, then simply move yourself away from that person and find the world that meets your own.

Open Mind, Open Heart

Our minds have the ability to transcend a reflective state. When forced into transition and change, turbulent times will throw our thoughts out of sync and away from our quiet moments.

We have the power through the mind to elevate away from our individual limitations. Thoughts bring calmness and clarity when steered away from the mind and guided by the heart.

Our minds have the potential to expand and surpass limitation when perception is eliminated and we let go of what we think. Then we can move more into what we feel.

An open mind means keeping an open mind-set. One's view of life should not be limited to right or wrong. It's the mix bag known as perception that allows us variety, as well as spice, to being individuals. This formulates our own uniqueness governed through thought, allowing the opportunity to present our personal views, which should not be judged by others.

OPPORTUNITY

I am whole, happy, and content with my life. Today, I believe in my own goodness and motivate myself to move beyond contentment to create new avenues for my life that will lead me to a deeper understanding of life and the world I live in. To keep myself from feeling stagnant, I will challenge myself with new opportunities that may seem difficult but will allow me to move myself past the humdrum of my existence. To find these new opportunities, I will start with finding something new of interest and I will pursue this venture with the intent of learning something new about myself.

To walk in fear is to walk in resistance.

To be confused in anger is to flounder in arrogance.

To babble of dissatisfaction is to live in noise.

To live in disappointment is to live in lack of self-awareness.

Repetition of negative behavior is a lack of respect for life.

*H*ealthy choices are the choices that lead us down a path of learning. The higher path of life is to make a healthy choice with each decision presented. However, one may need to take the road of bad choices to find what is healthy for them.

$\mathscr{I}$f something drives you to it, figure out what is there for you to learn before you turn your back and walk away.

For all that is dark, there will inevitably be light.

If you find you are caught in ebb, let your patience lead you to the flow.

There isn't a human being upon this earth that shall be exempt from the rollercoaster called life.

$\mathcal{H}$ang on to your beliefs, for they eventually lead you somewhere.

*W*orry is emotion wasted on moments of important growth; it is a bothersome emotion that falsely carries us through our darkest moments while laboring us with unwanted concern. If we were able to live through a situation without worry, we would feel free in those uncomfortable moments.

*W*hen struggling with the same situation, drop the rope. Take yourself out of play and let whatever is to happen, happen. You will feel much better when you let go of the struggle.

*L*aughter: the light vibration of soul that lies deep within our soul. Ignited with a moment of earthly pleasure, laughter is the gift we are given just for being human.

$\mathcal{W}$here there is shadow, there is light.

Where there is light, there is shadow.

Where there is life, there is choice.

Harboring anger only creates frustration and confusion in the mind. Friction ignites unwarranted uncertainties and triggers our insecurities. Forgiveness relieves the heaviness that is bound in the heart. Choose wisely with your responses to your daily situations. The outcome will rest in your ability to move your personality out of false pride and evaluate your responses, moving from ego into the heart of emotion.

Marbles

Compassion, strength, courage, toys, books, and trinkets—the treasures of life are all in the perception of the seeker.

Find your passion in life by connecting to your joys, moments of contentment that provide you with a sense of ideas and ideals.

A pocket full of marbles is just as meaningful as a pocket full of crystals. If one can be open to all opportunities and hold intent to try, life will be no less than adventurous.

*C*reativity is something that moves through us, not something that comes from us.

A kaleidoscope shows us an illumination of shapes, figures, and color. An energy field is as brilliant as the kaleidoscope transformed into brilliant patterns that are seen through the eyes of the viewer, though only a few choose to open their vision enough to see it.

FAITH

We never know when it is going to happen; we just have to remain open that our creations are a forward movement set forth in the universe. Trusting whatever is in our highest good will happen—just in God's time, not ours. We just have to continue trying and let the powers that be continue to work in our favor.

$\mathcal{T}$he difference between a guru and yourself is that they have mastered the ability to edify their commitment to their spirituality and faith.

The presence of God lives in our faith. No human can change the truth of our beliefs. Neither can another challenge what we believe based on opinions. When we stand strong in our convictions, we are not to challenge another. Just simply stay true to your design around your individual choices of God, the universe, and spirituality. Others can only offer their insight as an exchange.

*C*reating change in life means putting effort into your day to day.

It means persistence even when the doors continue to close with your every attempt.

It means courage to step into an unknown arena filled with uncertainty.

It means effort when you feel all attempts are lost.

Trust that every moment has value.

When someone has a faith that is strong, why banter that your faith is better? Just accept that the combination of both in some universal way brings harmony and balance to the collective.

*W*e are all born with a purpose; no life is grander than the other. Tap into your inner silence and quiet your mind long enough to believe that no one person has your direction in mind. Say aloud, "Powers that be, simply guide me." Trusting in the unseen will bring you everlasting hope that the purpose you seek is in the exact direction you are heading. Looking toward the heavens will not give you the insight. Rather, believing in the heavens will fill you with the drive to move yourself forward.

We are not here to sacrifice; we are here upon this earth to learn. Sacrifice comes only in the letting go of our perceptions of failure and our acceptance of lessons. Life is the gift God has given without the judgment of wrongfulness. Life is blessed because it is in our living that we shall learn. Until the day does come for us to part this earthly plane, then it will be that day we will be able to say, "I have done my best, and my failures have given me grace throughout this lifelong journey." Until that day, feel blessed with every moment.

*F*inding peace with each moment means believing in yourself; there is no power greater than being in human form. No existence is more fulfilling than the gift of life. If you are lacking in the true meaning of life, then life is challenging you to turn yourself towards finding a faith.

The universe is full of untapped resources, abundant treasures that exist on the other side of the veil. We all have the power to tap into this divine resource. We have all come directly from the source, and therefore we have the ability to tap into it. The only difference between one human and another is one's ability to believe in the world that is unseen.

The foundation of truth is faith. The foundation of faith is trust. To find the foundation of self, you must trust in your faith.

*W*hen we live our life on the whim of our personality, we will continually feel frustrated. If we trust in the world of the unknown, we can find solace in the unseen and then let go of frustration.

I let go of my fears and trust in the process that is unfolding. My thoughts may wander in and out of worry. May my faith never waver in the most unstable of situations. I ground my fears by silencing, because I know I will be taken care of, for this is in my divine plan.

Freedom arrives in life through the choices we make. If we choose openness, we choose a life of flow. If we choose a life of fear filled with blame, we choose a life with limits. If we choose a life lived in faith, we are forever open to possibilities.

*W*hen you find yourself continually hitting a wall, change your focus. Let the unknown take care of your life.

Anger can turn itself in to an unwarranted cyclone that leaves the creator looking unhealthy in his or her individual storm.

*I*f you are not participating in your life, it means you are not giving God gratitude for your creation.

Humankind

Through others we have the potential to learn. Some lessons are good, and others may be perceived as bad. Some may leave us happy, but some may have us feeling sad.

With the outer world all around, it's natural to view our reflection of self through the mirror image of others. Through the conversations we share and the mistakes we make, from the way we dress, to those who try and be the best. On one level or another, we energetically fail to get the lesson.

No truth is too strong, and no words are too late. If we are aware that we are all connected, it's easier to appreciate the gift of others.

Respect the value of others, because it teaches us that they are here to help us understand ourselves as individuals.

The collective consciousness is designed as a community of souls coming together collectively and subconsciously, to generate a lifetime of unconditional love through lessons in human form.

We are here to teach others how to live a dutiful life by being who we truly are as a single person, co-creating with others.

It is through others that we are able to find our individual selves.

*T*he power to manifest never slips away. The lag time between attracting and manifesting is not reflective of our abilities; it's just a moment to trust that all things happen in their own time.

There is always a solution for every problem—it just may not be the solution you were looking for. To be comfortable with what is given, you need to learn to live with an open mind.

Connecting to one's faith can be challenging when the world outside is pressuring you to give into your failures. Striving to see the light when all is dark leaves one feeling submissive to their moments of shadow. Hidden behind the darkness is the glimmer of hope we know as faith. Trust that this moment is only a moment and through the bleakness is a ray of light—even when you cannot see it.

There is no time in essence when you find yourself impatiently forcing a situation. Remind yourself the winds of heaven are in play. Things happen when they are supposed to. We are reminded to put forth the motion and trust that when something is meant to happen, it will happen not a moment too soon.

*S*elf-healing started long before we arrived on this planet we call earth. To continue one's inner healing process, one must become a stronger conduit and connect with one's own divine light.

SUCCESS

A life lived in happiness is a life lived in constant movement and positive pursuit.

*M*agic is performed by a magician. Healing is not magic; it is simply the ability to connect to love from a source greater than self. The truth is never hidden when one is connected to the flow of universal energy known as love and light.

*M*oney can always be made, but health can never be restored.

All doors open when we gently close the old ones. Taking an action toward opening a door means accepting that one door may need to be closed.

Perseverance has not been one of the stronger aspects of my personality. Resistance is more a part of me. Strength is a blessing I would like to acquire; it is a more courageous attempt at finding my true self and fulfilling my life's desires.

*L*ife means forgiveness for all that goes undone.

*M*oney is the green energy of the universe that provides us with an opportunity to participate on this human plane. Defining a life through its worth only defines one's limitations. Living a life of abundance means being in the flow of one's green energy without attachment to limitation.

$\mathcal{F}$alling under the spiritual radar means you have dipped below your own glory. To raise yourself to the light, you have to concentrate on your abilities to succeed and not on the failures that sit before you.

*T*he key to success is not to look for success. Find something that you can personally invest time in enjoying and keep working at it.

*W*hen we circle round and round with our thoughts and words, we limit our ambitions and become stale and stagnant, with no ability to move.

$\mathcal{S}$uccess can only come when one focuses on staying in the moment and redefining that moment, building upon each moment of the day.

Creativity and passion create a person's core vision of self. Before one can find a deeper level of connection to self, one must tap into their desires. Desires live in the essence of the human soul. No desire will ever be found by seeking with the mind. The only way to find one's true desire begins with connection to self through the heart.

Life is truly all our creation. Our accomplishments are those we choose to tackle. One must find something that stimulates and challenges one's personality. Successes lie in our ability to motivate ourselves and follow through with action. Motivation begins with the acknowledgement that every action has purpose. Even within failure, we can find movement.

*M*ost people fail when their goals are geared toward perfection. A lack of patience will turn the personality toward frustration. Some become disappointed due to the attachment that is formed around an outcome. Others are successful when they put forth an action and remain in their belief that all happens as it should. There are no failures, only lessons.

*H*appiness takes work because life is a challenge. Everything in life that is work creates happiness. Move through the moments knowing everything created through challenge will create happiness.

Finding joy in your life means you will have to let go of the rigidity. Nothing in life is accomplished through control.

*W*ishing for a life of riches, love, and comfort isn't enough to fulfill the wish. One must put forth the effort to manifest such desires. Manifesting means putting into action a life of dedication, commitment, and drive. Only then will you be able to have all those things you long to have in life.

Simple Observation

Throughout my life, I have had many experiences with others in which I can recall moments of viewing kind, mindful, tender acts of human awareness. They were generous tones of thoughtful human kindness.

I have observed some seriously harsh, unbearably arrogant gestures by some who were less thoughtful. Some of these moments have stirred emotions not fit for the human mind.

The outer world can be a simple reflection of goodness or a seedy reflection of darkness. Some people will choose to live their life one way, and others will choose the opposite.

The only way to live in the comfort of a life designed for you is to take in the view of life that suits your journey. Let the other view be one which you bear witness to and in which you choose not to partake in.

Sometimes observing what is happening in the outer world gives you the impetus to choose the life that suits you best.

So Mote It Be.

9 781452 535272